120 GREAT PAINTINGS OF
LOVE & ROMANCE

CD-ROM & Book

Edited by
Carol Belanger Grafton

Dover Publications, Inc.
Mineola, New York

The CD-ROM in this book contains all of the images. Each image has been saved as a 300-dpi high-resolution JPEG and a 72-dpi Internet-ready JPEG. There is no installation necessary. Just insert the CD into your computer and call the images into your favorite software (refer to the documentation with your software for further instructions).

Within the "Images" folder on the CD you will find two additional folders—"High Resolution JPG" and "JPG." Every image has a unique file name in the following format: xxx.JPG. The first 3 characters of the file name correspond to the number printed with the image in the book. The last 3 letters of the file name, JPG, refer to the file format. So, 001.JPG would be the first file in the folder.

Also included on the CD-ROM is Dover Design Manager, a simple graphics editing program for Windows that will allow you to view, print, crop, and rotate the images.

For technical support, contact:
Telephone: 1 (617) 249-0245
Fax: 1 (617) 249-0245
Email: dover@artimaging.com
Internet: **http://www.dovertechsupport.com**
The fastest way to receive technical support is via email or the Internet.

Bibliographical Note

120 Great Paintings of Love and Romance CD-ROM and Book, is a new work, originally published by Dover Publications, Inc., in 2010.

Dover Electronic Clip Art®

International Standard Book Number

ISBN-13: 978-0-486-99039-2
ISBN-10: 0-486-99039-7

Manufactured in the United States by Courier Corporation
99039701
www.doverpublications.com

001. Jacopo Amigoni
The Meeting of Habrokomes and Antheia; 1743–44

002. Thomas Hart Benton
Romance; 1931–32

004. Pierre Bonnard
Man and Woman; 1906

003. Arnold Böchlin
Springtime of Love; 1868–69

005. Paris Bordon
Venus, Mars, and Cupid Crowned by Victory; c. 1550

006. Sandro Botticelli
The Birth of Venus; c. 1484

007. SANDRO BOTTICELLI
Venus and Mars; c. 1485

008. FRANÇOIS BOUCHER
La Cible D'Amour (Love Target); 1758

010. FRANÇOIS BOUCHER
A Pastoral Landscape with a Shepherd and Shepherdess seated by Ruins; c. 1730

009. FRANÇOIS BOUCHER
Hercules and Omphale; c. 1731–34

012. ADOLPHE-WILLIAM BOUGUEREAU
The Birth of Venus; 1879

011. ADOLPHE-WILLIAM BOUGUEREAU
Young Girl Defending Herself Against Eros; c. 1880

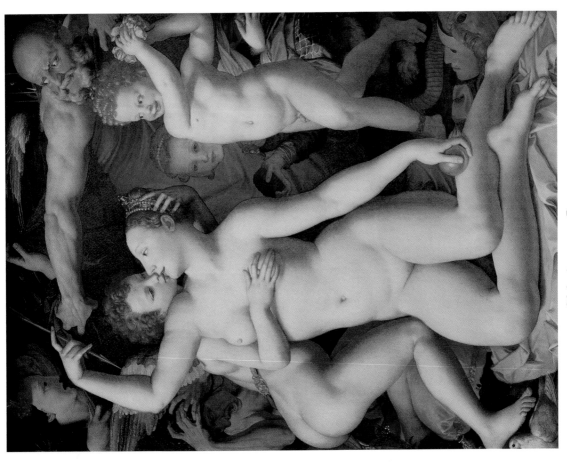

014. AGNOLO BRONZINO
An Allegory of Venus and Cupid; c. 1545

013. ADOLPHE-WILLIAM BOUGUEREAU
The Proposal; 1872

016. Sir Edward Burne-Jones
The Baleful Head; 1886–87

015. Ford Madox Brown
Romeo and Juliet; c. 1867

018. PHILIP HERMOGENES CALDERON
Broken Vows; 1856

017. SIR EDWARD BURNE-JONES
The Beguiling of Merlin; 1874

019. Domenico di Bernardino Caprioli
A Pair of Lovers and a Pilgrim in a Landscape; n.d.

020. Paul Cézanne
Afternoon in Naples; c. 1876

022. THE HONOURABLE JOHN COLLIER
In the Venusburg (Tannhäuser); 1901

021. JOHN S. CLIFTON
Love; c. 1850

023. CORREGGIO
Leda and Swan; c. 1531–32

024. CORREGGIO
Danaë; c. 1531–32

026. Pierre-August Cot
The Storm; 1880

025. Correggio
The Education of Cupid; c. 1528

028. LUCAS CRANACH THE ELDER
Cupid Complaining to Venus; c. 1525

027. LUCAS CRANACH THE ELDER
Samson and Delilah; c. 1529

029. Jacques-Louis David
The Farewell of Telemachus and Eucharis; 1818

030. Jacques-Louis David
Sappho and Phaon; 1809

031. Dosso Dossi
Circe and Her Lovers in a Landscape; c. 1511–12

032. William Dyce
Paolo and Francesca; 1837

033. Sir Anthony van Dyck
Cupid and Psyche; 1638–40

034. Charles-Dominique-Joseph Eisen
Cupid; n.d.

035. WILLIAM ETTY
Hero and Leander; 1828–29

036. JAN VAN EYCK
Portrait of Giovanni Arnolfini and His Wife; 1434

038. JEAN-HONORÉ FRAGONARD
The Declaration of Love; 1773

037. JEAN-FRANÇOIS DE TROY
The Declaration of Love; 1735

039. JEAN-HONORÉ FRAGONARD
The Happy Lovers; c. 1770

040. JEAN-HONORÉ FRAGONARD
The Stolen Kiss; c. 1785–90

041. MARCANTONIO FRANCESCHINI
Venus Anointing the Dead Adonis; 1692–1700

042. BARON FRANCOIS GERARD
Psyche Receiving the First Kiss of Love; 1798

044. LUCA GIORDANO
Acis and Galatea; c. 1685

045. HENDRICK GOLTZIUS
The Fall of Man; 1616

046. CORNELIS CORNELISZOON VAN HAARLEM
A Courting Couple and a Woman with a Songbook; c. 1594

049. Arthur Hughes
The Brave Geraint (Geraint and Enid); c. 1860

050. Arthur Hughes
The Long Engagement; 1853–59

051. WILLIAM HOLMAN HUNT
Valentine Rescuing Sylvia from Proteus; 1850–51

052. WILLIAM HOLMAN HUNT
The Hireling Shepherd; 1851–52

054. JEAN-AUGUSTE-DOMINIQUE INGRES
Paolo and Francesca; 1819

053. WILLIAM HOLMAN HUNT
The Awakening Conscience; 1853

056. JEAN-AUGUSTE-DOMINIQUE INGRES
Jupiter and Thetis; 1811

055. JEAN-AUGUSTE-DOMINIQUE INGRES
Raphael and the Fornarina; 1811–12

057. Angelica Kauffman
Cephalus with Procris and Cupid; n.d.

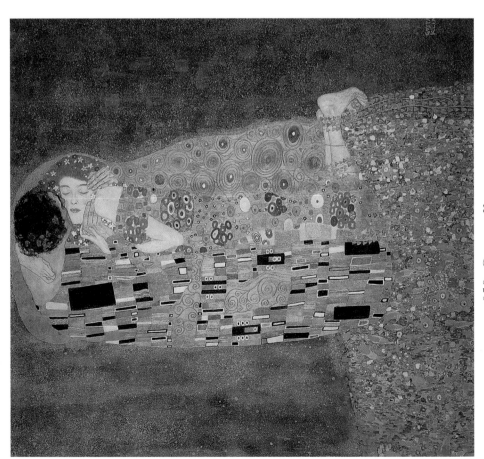

058. Gustav Klimt
The Kiss; 1907–08

059. Oskar Kokoschka
The Bride of the Wind (The Tempest); 1914

060. George Cochran Lambdin
The Courtship; 1864–65

062. TAMARA DE LEMPICKA
Adam and Eve; 1932

061. FRANÇOIS LE MOYNE
Hercules and Omphale; 1724

064. Pietro Longhi
The Married Couple's Breakfast; 1744

065. Lorenzo Lotto
Venus and Cupid; c. 1525

066. Lorenzo Lotto
Portrait of a Married Couple; c. 1523–24

067. KAREL VAN MANDER I
Garden of Love; 1600

068. SIR JOHN EVERETT MILLAIS
The Huguenot; 1851–52

069. GUSTAVE MOREAU
Galatea; 1880

070. CHARLES–JOSEPH NATOIRE
Venus and Cupid; c. 1745

072. SIR JOSEPH NOEL PATON
Hesperus; 1857

071. SIR JOSEPH NOEL PATON
The Bluidie Tryst; 1855

073. GIOVANNI ANTONIO PELLEGRINI
Venus and Cupid; n.d.

074. PABLO PICASSO
The Lovers; 1923

076. ANTONIO DEL POLLAIUOLO
Apollo and Daphne; c. 1460

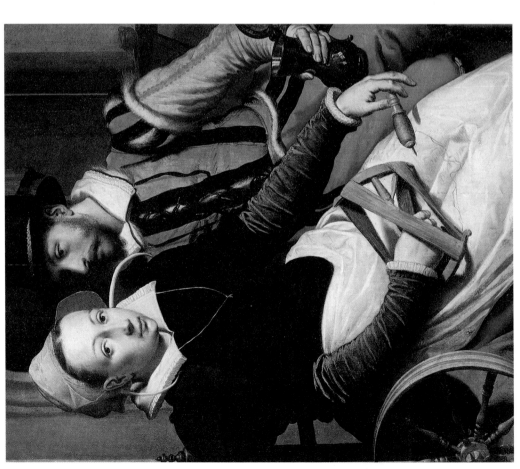

075. PIETER PIETERSZ
Man and Woman at a Spinning Wheel; c. 1570

077. Rembrandt van Rijn
The Bridal Couple; c. 1665

078. Pierre-Auguste Renoir
Dance in the Country; 1883

080. SEBASTIANO RICCI
The Punishment of Love; 1706–07

079. JOSHUA REYNOLDS
Cupid Untying the Zone of Venus; 1788

082. Giulio Romano
Two Lovers; c. 1524

084. DANTE GABRIEL ROSSETTI
St. George and the Princess Sabra; 1862

083. DANTE GABRIEL ROSSETTI
The Wedding of St. George and the Princess Sabra; 1857

086. PETER PAUL RUBENS
Rubens and Isabella Brant Under a Honeysuckle Bower; 1609–10

085. DANTE GABRIEL ROSSETTI
The Beloved (The Bride); 1865–66

087. PETER PAUL RUBENS
The Garden of Love; c. 1630–32

088. PETER PAUL RUBENS
Samson and Delilah; c. 1609–10

089. PETER PAUL RUBENS
Venus and Adonis; c. 1635

090. JOHN SINGER SARGENT
Paul Helleu Sketching with His Wife; 1889

092. SIMEON SOLOMON
Sappho and Erinna in a Garden at Mitylene; 1864

093. JOHN RODDAM SPENCER-STANHOPE
Love and the Maiden; 1877

094. CARL SPITZWEG
The Love Letter; 1845–46

096. Jan Steen
The Seduction; c. 1668–72

095. Bartholomeus Spranger
Venus and Adonis; c. 1597

098. GERARD TERBORCH
The Suitor's Visit; c. 1658

097. GERARD TERBORCH
A Woman Playing the Theorbo-Lute and a Cavalier; c. 1658

099. GIAMBATTISTA TIEPOLO
Apollo Pursuing Daphne; c. 1755–60

100. TITIAN
Venus Blindfolding Cupid; c. 1565

101. TITIAN
Venus With a Mirror; c. 1555

102. TITIAN
Bacchus and Ariadne; c. 1523

103. TITIAN
Venus and Adonis; 1555–60

104. HENRI DE TOULOUSE-LAUTREC
The Kiss; 1893

105. JOSEPH MALLORD WILLIAM TURNER
Venus and Adonis; c. 1803–05

106. JOHN VANDERLYN
Ariadne Asleep on the Island of Naxos; 1809–14

107. DIEGO VELÁZQUEZ
Venus at Her Mirror (The Rokeby Venus); c. 1644–48

108. JAN VERKOLJE
An Elegant Couple with Musical Instruments in an Interior; 1671–74

110. Simon Vouet
Venus and Adonis; c. 1642

109. Paolo Veronese
Mars and Venus United by Love; c. 1570

112. JOHN WILLIAM WATERHOUSE
Apollo and Daphne; 1908

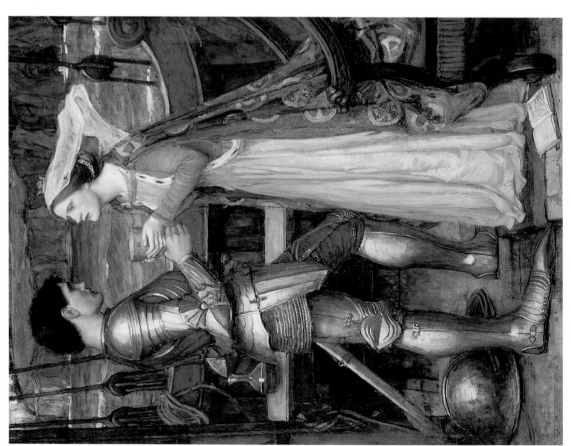

111. JOHN WILLIAM WATERHOUSE
Tristram and Isolde; 1916

113. JOHN WILLIAM WATERHOUSE
The Awakening of Adonis; c. 1900

114. JOHN WILLIAM WATERHOUSE
Lamia; 1905

116. JOHN WILLIAM WATERHOUSE
The Siren; c. 1900

115. JOHN WILLIAM WATERHOUSE
La Belle Dame Sans Merci; 1893

117. Benjamin West
Cupid and Psyche; 1808

118. Benjamin West
Portrait of Mr. and Mrs. John Custance; 1778

120. ANONYMOUS
A Bridal Pair; c. 1470

119. JOACHIM WTEWAEL
Perseus Rescuing Andromeda; 1611

LIST OF WORKS

059. Oskar Kokoschka (1886–1980); *The Bride of the Wind (The Tempest)*; 1914; oil on canvas; 71¼" x 86⅝" (181 x 220 cm)

060. George Cochran Lambdin (1830–1896); *The Courtship*; 1864–65; oil on canvas; 22" x 18" (55.8 x 45.7 cm)

061. François Le Moyne (1688–1737); *Hercules and Omphale*; 1724; oil on canvas; 72½" x 58½" (184 x 149 cm)

062. Tamara de Lempicka (1898–1980); *Adam and Eve*; 1932; oil on cardboard; 46½" x 29⅛" (118 x 74 cm)

063. Fra Filippo Lippi (1406–1469); *Portrait of a Woman and a Man at a Casement*; c. 1440–44; tempera on panel; 25¼" x 16½" (64.1 x 41.9 cm)

064. Pietro Longhi (c. 1702–1785); *The Married Couple's Breakfast*; 1744; oil on canvas; 19¼" x 23½" (49 x 60 cm)

065. Lorenzo Lotto (c. 1480–1556); *Venus and Cupid*; c. 1525; oil on canvas; 36⅞" x 43⅞" (92.4 x 111.4 cm)

066. Lorenzo Lotto (c. 1480–1556); *Portrait of a Married Couple*; c. 1523–24; oil on canvas; 37⅞" x 45¾" (96 x 116.2 cm)

067. Karel van Mander I (1548–1606); *Garden of Love*; 1600; oil on canvas; 18" x 27½" (45 x 70 cm)

068. Sir John Everett Millais (1829–1896); *The Huguenot*; 1851–52; oil on canvas; 36½" x 25¼" (93 x 64 cm)

069. Gustave Moreau (1826–1898); *Galatea*; 1880; oil on panel; 33⅝" x 26⅜"(85 x 67 cm)

070. Charles-Joseph Natoire (1700–1777); *Venus and Cupid*; c. 1745; oil on canvas; 43¼" x 53⅜" (110 x 135.5 cm)

071. Sir Joseph Noel Paton (1821–1901); *The Bluidie Tryst*; 1855; oil on canvas; 28¾" x 25⅝" (73 x 65 cm)

072. Sir Joseph Noel Paton (1821–1901); *Hesperus*; 1857; oil on canvas; 36" x 27" (91 x 69 cm)

073. Giovanni Antonio Pellegrini (1675–1741); *Venus and Cupid*; n.d.; oil on canvas; 40½" x 49¾" (103 x 126.5 cm)

074. Pablo Picasso (1881–1973); *The Lovers*; 1923; oil on canvas; 51¼" x 38¼" (130.2 x 97.2 cm)

075. Pieter Pietersz (c. 1540–1603); *Man and Woman at a Spinning Wheel*; c. 1570; oil on panel; 30" x 20⅞"(76 x 53 cm)

076. Antonio del Pollaiuolo (1431–1498); *Apollo and Daphne*; c. 1460; oil on panel; 11½" x 7¾" (29.5 x 20 cm)

077. Rembrandt van Rijn (1606–1669); *The Bridal Couple*; c. 1665; oil on canvas; 47¾" x 65½" (121.5 x 166.3 cm)

078. Pierre-Auguste Renoir (1841–1919); *Dance in the Country*; 1883; oil on canvas; 70⅞" x 35½" (180 x 90 cm)

079. Joshua Reynolds (1723–1792); *Cupid Untying the Zone of Venus*; 1788; oil on canvas; 50⅛" x 39¾" (127.3 x 100.9 cm)

080. Sebastiano Ricci (1659–1734); *The Punishment of Love*; 1706–07; oil on canvas; 112¼" x 112¼" (285 x 285 cm)

081. Louis-Léopold Robert (1794–1835); *A Girl from Procida*; 1822; oil on canvas; 31¾"x 27" (81 x 68.5 cm)

082. Giulio Romano (1499–1546); *Two Lovers*; c. 1524; oil on canvas; 64⅛" x 131⅝" (163 x 337 cm)

083. Dante Gabriel Rossetti (1828–1882); *The Wedding of St. George and the Princess Sabra*; 1857; watercolor on paper; 13½" x 13½" (34 x 34 cm)

084. Dante Gabriel Rossetti (1828–1882); *St. George and the Princess Sabra*; 1862; watercolor on paper; 20⅝" x 12⅛" (52.4 x 30.8 cm)

085. Dante Gabriel Rossetti (1828–1882); *The Beloved (The Bride)*; 1865–66; oil on canvas; 32½" x 30" (82.5 x 76.2 cm)

086. Peter Paul Rubens (1577–1640); *Rubens and Isabella Brant Under a Honeysuckle Bower*; 1609–10; oil on canvas; 70⅛" x 53¾" (178 x 136.5 cm)

087. Peter Paul Rubens (1577–1640); *The Garden of Love*; c. 1630–32; oil on canvas; 77⅛" x 111⅜" (198 x 283 cm)

088. Peter Paul Rubens (1577–1640); *Samson and Delilah*; c. 1609–10; oil on panel; 72¾"x 80¾" (185 x 205 cm)

089. Peter Paul Rubens (1577–1640); *Venus and Adonis*; c. 1635; oil on canvas; 77¾" x 95⅝" (197.4 x 242.8 cm)

090. John Singer Sargent (1856–1925); *Paul Helleu Sketching with His Wife*; 1889; oil on canvas; 26⅛" x 32⅛" (66.3 x 81.5 cm)

091. Jan van Scorel (1495–1562); *Adam and Eve*; c. 1540; oil on panel; 18¾" x 12½" (47.6 x 31.8 cm)

092. Simeon Solomon (1840–1905); *Sappho and Erinna in a Garden at Mitylene*; 1864; watercolor on paper; 13" x 15" (33 x 38.1 cm)

093. John Roddam Spencer-Stanhope (1829–1908); *Love and the Maiden*; 1877; oil on canvas; 54¼" x 79¾" (138 x 201 cm)

094. Carl Spitzweg (1808–1885); *The Love Letter*; 1845–46; oil on canvas; 9½" x 8¼" (24.1 x 20.9 cm)

095. Bartholomeus Spranger (1546–1611); *Venus and Adonis*; c. 1597; oil on canvas; 64" x 41" (163 x 104 cm)

096. Jan Steen (1626–1679); *The Seduction*; c. 1668–72; oil on panel; 19¼" x 15½" (49 x 39.5 cm)

097. Gerard Terborch (1617–1681); *A Woman Playing the Theorbo-Lute and a Cavalier*; c. 1658; oil on wood; 14½" x 12¾" (36.8 x 32.4 cm)

098. Gerard Terborch (1617–1681); *The Suitor's Visit*; c. 1658; oil on canvas; 31½" x 29⅝" (80 x 75 cm)

099. Giambattista Tiepolo (1696–1770); *Apollo Pursuing Daphne*; c. 1755–60; oil on canvas; 27" x 34¼" (68.5 x 87)

100. Titian (c. 1488–1576); *Venus Blindfolding Cupid*; c. 1565; oil on canvas; 45⅝" x 72½" (116 x 184 cm)

101. Titian (c. 1488–1576); *Venus With a Mirror*; c. 1555; oil on canvas; 49" x 41½" (124.5 x 105.5 cm)

102. Titian (c. 1488–1576); *Bacchus and Ariadne*; c. 1523; oil on canvas; 69½" x 75¼" (176.5 x 191cm)

103. Titian (c. 1488–1576); *Venus and Adonis*; 1555–60; oil on canvas; 63" x 77⅜" (160 x 196.5 cm)

104. Henri de Toulouse-Lautrec (1864–1901); *The Kiss*; 1893; oil on canvas; 15⅜" x 22¾" (39 x 58 cm)

105. Joseph Mallord William Turner (1775–1851); *Venus and Adonis*; c. 1803–05; oil on canvas; 59" x 47" (149.9 x 119.4 cm)

106. John Vanderlyn (1775–1852); *Ariadne Asleep on the Island of Naxos*; 1809–14; oil on canvas; 68½" x 87" (174.1 x 221.1 cm)

107. Diego Velázquez (1599–1660); *Venus at Her Mirror (The Rokeby Venus)*; c. 1644–48; oil on canvas; 48¼" x 69⅝" (122.5 x 177 cm)

108. Jan Verkolje (1650–1693); *An Elegant Couple with Musical Instruments in an Interior*; 1671–74; oil on canvas; 38" x 32¼" (96.5 x 82 cm)

109. Paolo Veronese (c. 1528–1588); *Mars and Venus United by Love*; c. 1570; oil on canvas; 81" x 63⅜" (205.7 x 161 cm)

110. Simon Vouet (1590–1649); *Venus and Adonis*; c. 1642; oil on canvas; 51¼" x 37¼" (130 x 94.5 cm)

111. John William Waterhouse (1849–1917); *Tristram and Isolde*; 1916; oil on canvas; 42" x 32" (107.5 x 81.5 cm)

112. John William Waterhouse (1849–1917); *Apollo and Daphne*; 1908; oil on canvas; 57" x 44⅛" (145 x 112 cm)

113. John William Waterhouse (1849–1917); *The Awakening of Adonis*; c. 1900; oil on canvas; 37¾" x 74" (95.9 x 188 cm)

114. John William Waterhouse (1849–1917); *Lamia*; 1905; oil on canvas; 57" x 36" (144.7 x 91.4 cm)

115. John William Waterhouse (1849–1917); *La Belle Dame Sans Merci*; 1893; oil on canvas; 44" x 32" (112 x 81 cm)

116. John William Waterhouse (1849–1917); *The Siren*; c. 1900; oil on canvas; 31⅞" x 20⅞" (81 x 53 cm)

117. Benjamin West (1738–1820); *Cupid and Psyche*; 1808; oil on canvas; 54¼" x 56¼" (137.8 x 142.5 cm)

118. Benjamin West (1738–1820); *Portrait of Mr. and Mrs. John Custance*; 1778; oil on canvas; 83" x 59" (210.8 x 149.9 cm)

119. Joachim Wtewael (1566–1638); *Perseus Rescuing Andromeda*; 1611; oil on canvas; 71" x 59" (180 x 150 cm)

120. Anonymous; *A Bridal Pair*; c. 1470; tempera on wood; 24½" x 14⅜" (62.3 x 36.5 cm)